Dear and inquisitive readers, I am very glad that YOU are developing and improving your skills.

Knowledge will give you power, but good character will give you respect.

GREETINGS, MY FRIEND AND READER, IT IS MY GREAT PLEASURE TO SHARE MY OBSERVATIONS WITH YOU.

nice to meet you!

The book is written in a way that you will read it easily and quickly. Otherwise, lengthy discussions from psychology probably won't be necessary for you, and you'll find concrete advice more useful, which you can immediately apply in your work.

In my opinion, the best sales guide is one that you can read in a day or two and that will immediately help you achieve better results. I believe that the book in front of you is exactly that kind. I would be glad if you let me know what you think about it and if it helped you in any way.

This book does not offer a miraculous and all-powerful remedy and does not promise you an instant turnaround in your sales career. I believe that without your efforts and a desire to achieve the best sales results, no book can work miracles.

You can use this book as an effective tool to identify and correct the most common and annoying sales mistakes that unnecessarily eat into your income. If you're interested, read the book.

creator: Sergii **Ka**

In my firm belief, sales is the most exciting business in the world. When organized correctly, it offers you virtually unlimited earning potential, freedom, and the ability to effectively manage your career and life as a whole. In this regard, I believe that the profession of a salesperson far surpasses any other professional activity. However, sales, unfortunately, are not without their challenges.

In seminars, the first question we ask salespeople is: "What changes would you most like to see in your job?" We always receive the same answer to this question: "We would like to see a change in people's attitudes toward our work."

People often simply do not trust salespeople. This is partly due to bad experiences with brokers and partly due to the distorted image of salespeople in the media. Whether it is a not-so-honest used car salesperson or a crafty dealer committing some crime, the media never portray salespeople as hardworking, responsible, and honest professionals. Instead, negative stereotypes closely associated with the sales profession are repeated countless times every day.

Always draw conclusions from the mistakes you have made, analyze and move on to victory with the experience you have already gained.

Indeed, there are many salespeople around us who would like to make a quick profit by exploiting people's trust, and at every step, we encounter brokers who loudly praise their goods and care little about satisfying their customers. But this book will not help such traders because it is intended for honest salespeople like you, who strive to establish good business contacts and achieve the best results. In short, it is for those who also stand behind what they sell. But what does a potential buyer think of us when we knock on their door? Perhaps they think of those brokers who talk too fast for people to understand and who whistle about opinions to those who might fall for them. Occasionally, we fail to sell something not because of our own mistakes, but because of the mistakes of those who came before us.

This book will help you demonstrate the professionalism and sense of responsibility that are indispensable qualities for a salesperson's success today. It will reveal to you twenty-five techniques of successful business people that will help you stand out day and night from the "amateur" salespeople who might confuse you at first. This book will help you succeed in the most diverse and dynamic profession of our time.

Earlier, I emphasized that much has changed in the business world, especially in sales, since the late seventies or early eighties. Before we delve deeper into the proven techniques that lead to success, let's consider three of the most important facts that the modern salesperson must keep in mind at every stage.

The first and most important fact is that today your potential clients are more sensitive to the value of products or services than ever before, and they have access to significantly more up-to-date information than in the past. From the very first moment of meeting a new potential client, you must be ready to present the successes you have already achieved with other clients and have all the advantages of the products or services you offer at hand. You must approach the first meeting with a potential buyer with an enviable knowledge of your business sector. Of course, this does not mean that you have to memorize an entire encyclopedia before you can sell anything, nor that you have to persuade the potential buyer with beautiful but incomprehensible words. But nowadays, when time pressures us at every step and we are increasingly receptive to various kinds of information, you must convincingly show your interlocutor that your company possesses unique and extremely important knowledge and skills that can be beneficial to them.

Another fact, which may come as a surprise to many salespeople, is that convincing a potential buyer often requires a highly persuasive presentation that is not necessarily focused solely on the buyer's immediate needs. For decades, we have been taught to focus on these already defined "needs" of the potential buyer, but now it's about helping the buyer identify their needs and requirements, which are crucial for the seller today. This sometimes means asking the prospect about what they do, how, when, where, and why they do it, and, of course, how you can help them in their work, but only to meet their desires and needs.

Thirdly, a successful salesperson is ready to see the future, which means they always have an advantage. I mean the next step in the sales process. In short, they think about the future and how to retain existing clients. A good salesperson must skillfully avoid any unproductive conversations with potential buyers. Therefore, they must be prepared to change their outdated approach, which clearly no longer works, even if it may have been a very successful sales method in the past—looking forward means taking responsibility for their own career. For a true salesperson, someone who loves challenges and is ready to take full responsibility for their fate, this is not particularly difficult.

Make no mistake: you will have to work hard to attract and retain clients. Intense competition is a hallmark of the modern market. The time for complacency in sales is long gone, if it ever existed at all.

Many other salespeople are also competing for the business you are diligently trying to acquire. Some of them are very successful, earning a lot of money and securing enviable careers that can last several decades, while others make one or another fatal mistake and burn out. I have worked with both. This book describes proven techniques that successful businesspeople use in their work, and if you start using them too, they will surely be very useful to you.

I wish you good luck!

CON ARTIST 1

You convince people that they can trust you.

I have already trained over a quarter of a million salespeople, and I am increasingly noticing how some sellers try to take shortcuts using certain "sales tricks," thinking it will help them achieve their goals faster. The only problem is that most of these "sales tricks," or what could be called "dirty tricks," fail to accomplish the main task: consistently communicating and reinforcing the message that trusting these sellers is a good business decision.

The "trick" and its consequences in building long-term partnerships.

I know a car salesman who uses one of these "tricks" to lure people into his dealership. He opens a phone book, finds a random person, and says, "Good day, Mr. Jones. This is Mike from Johnson's Used Cars. I'm happy to share some good news: you've just won a turkey in a raffle. So, I'm asking you to contact us and collect your prize in person." Of course, he never reveals his true intention, which is for the lucky winner to take not just the turkey but a car as well.

I know a salesperson who repeatedly calls random people and boasts about finding their wallet just to grab their attention, hoping it will make them easier to convince to buy something. How can you trust someone who uses such tactics?

I don't want to be unfair to those businesspeople who make a living selling cars. Some of the most successful salespeople I know sell cars. But I'd like to add something else about the used car salesman who tried to attract customers with fabrications. He used a cheap trick to share the good news about the "turkey win" over the phone, and I don't think it's a coincidence that his car sales were not booming. Soon, people discovered the real motive behind his bait.

If you're selling turkeys, talk about turkeys; if you're selling cars, talk about cars. Instead, try to convince a potential customer without making noise about why your product or service is a particularly good fit for them, and avoid cheap "marketing tricks." If they come at the cost of your reputation, they'll be very expensive.

A successful salesperson is also a good leader because they inspire with the truth. I believe that truly successful salespeople, whom I consider to be the greatest masters of this profession in the world, stand out for their personal charm and the confidence with which they say to people, "Follow me!" This way, they gain loyal, satisfied customers. Such convincing authority is supported only by the client's complete and unwavering trust that you can offer them the best solutions. If you're right, customers trust you and follow you.

Thus, building trust also means developing leadership qualities. This doesn't mean you need to learn how to deceive your customers. All the trust and authority in the world won't change the fact that saying, "I found a wallet you never lost," doesn't build trust. It's about thoroughly knowing your product or service, so you know what your partner does and ensure full accountability to meet your customers' needs. In this case, potential customers will immediately understand what you offer, and they will like it.

What are the characteristics of a good leader?

A good leader has vision.
A good leader commands respect.
A good leader takes a holistic view of things.
A good leader knows when to change direction.
A good leader identifies problem areas and is ready to discuss possible solutions.
A good leader excels both in approach and in managing relationships.
A good leader takes responsibility.
All of these qualities, individually and collectively, contribute to genuine authority.

Too many salespeople strive to merely appear trustworthy, but that is not enough. You must earn trust with every word. I specifically mean accuracy. For example, if you promise to call someone at exactly nine o'clock, then actually call them at nine, not two minutes later. Even better, call a bit earlier and wait for them by the phone.

If you think that such "minor details" are insignificant and won't help build trust, you are deeply mistaken. At the very beginning of your interactions with a potential customer, these seemingly small "details" may be your only tool. If you make promises you can't keep, and if you fail to deliver on the aforementioned details, you will be no better than the vast majority of average salespeople. But if you promise a potential customer that you will send them a proposal by fax that fully meets their needs within the next five minutes and then actually do it, you will still just be one among thousands.

Relationships are built on mutual trust, and trust must be supported by a variety of proofs. Of course, this doesn't mean you should place yourself in a subordinate position that contradicts the role of a leader. You must demonstrate that you are unconditionally reliable in all aspects, both small and large, and you must develop the habit of delivering on your promises and, if possible, giving more of yourself. Only then will you be able to speak with true authority and conviction.

You are asking the right questions

Ask important yet relevant questions. You can start by helping yourself by asking about the weather or how your roommate is feeling, but beyond that, ask all questions based on a simple principle: never waste a potential buyer's time.

To many people this principle will seem completely obvious, but most sellers clearly don't see it that way. You need to know when it's the right time to switch from polite chatter about office equipment, sporting events, the weather and more to the business world. After all, you have come to a business meeting and your interlocutor would like to talk business too.
One question to help you get to the business part of the conversation.
How do you start asking the important questions? I suggest starting with a seemingly simple question that has nothing to do at first glance. be careful during your visit, but it will help you get to know the person you are talking to better.
"May I ask how you came to be in the business you are in?"
A question like this will surely ease the transition to the business part of the conversation, as well as loosen up your conversation partner's tongue. After he answers this question in as much detail as he deems necessary, you can go on with what you have in mind and explain the purpose of your visit.   For example like this:
"We deal in so-and-so products that have been a great success in sales all over the country. Let me tell you a little about my job.
My only purpose for this first visit is to get to know your business better. I'm not here to sell you anything today, I'm just pointing it out because I wanted to ask you some questions about your store and see if I can really help you increase your sales. Do you have enough time to talk about these things? "
And what do you do after you've told a potential customer a little bit about your business solutions?

Assuming the potential customer has answered the previous question in the affirmative, there is a good chance that this actually happened, then you can move on to the "big" questions.

(The first question is in the past tense:) "Have you ever used our products?" (If the answer is yes, you will of course ask how they did it).

(Second question is present tense:) "May I ask what products you are currently using instead of ours and how satisfied you are with them?"

(Third question is future:) "Tell me, what consumption of the products we're talking about do you predict in the next six months?" ("How are you going to use these products to achieve your goals?")

If you're not in the mood to jump right into serious questions about whether the person's company is already using your products or plans to use them in the near future, and you're still confident that you've moved beyond the initial soccer questions, you can help yourself with a series of intermediate questions that you'll ask before moving on to the main topic of conversation. Here are some suggestions:

" 'Tell me about the kind of customers you deal with?

"Does your company have any other branches or representative offices?"

(Or: "Where is your headquarters?").

"What is your sales method?"

"How long has your company been in this business?"

"What challenges are you currently facing in your business area?"

These and similar questions will help you gather important information, and can serve as a useful "bridge" to the most important point of your visit. But don't worry too much about these transient questions because, in all likelihood, your contact is short on time, as is the case with all of us these days. Most potential buyers will appreciate it if you answer key questions as quickly as possible that won't jeopardize the success of your business.

The last "real" question you ask on your first visit will usually go something like this:

"Mr. Jones, I have to tell you that I learned a lot of interesting and useful things today, and I want to thank you for giving me so much of your valuable time. Let me tell you something that I usually say in a case like this:,,,,,,,,,,, I think we are getting to the point where I will have to make another appointment with you. Then, because of all I have learned today, I will show you clearly what I can do for your company on Tuesday at three o'clock, or at noon?"

You Take the Initiative

Keep the potential client informed about your progress at any stage of the sales cycle. Don't hesitate to steer the conversation in the direction you need.

You could start with something like this:

"Mr. Jones, I want to extend my sincere thanks for giving me so much of your time. I know we have a lot to discuss, but during this part of the visit, I usually provide some information about my company and what we do. We've been producing this product for many years..."

"Mr. Jones, at this point in the conversation, I'd like to ask a few simple questions to help me find the best way to assist you."

"Mr. Jones, now that we've reached this stage in our discussion, I'm going to tell you what I plan to do next. I'd like to take a few notes about your company's business, and then I'll head back to my office and do my best to prepare a suitable proposal for you as soon as possible. How about we meet again next week? For example, would Friday at 2 PM work for you?"

"It would certainly be helpful for us to meet again, Mr. Jones. We've prepared a proposal specifically for you, and, if you don't mind, I'd like to take five minutes to briefly go over its features and then answer any questions you may have."

"Mr. Jones, here is our proposal. I hope we can meet your expectations in every respect. We believe that it would be in the best interest of you and your company if we proceed with our plans as soon as possible. Do you think Saturday, December 12th, would be a good day to get started?"

The Dangers of "Hurting" a Potential Customer

How many presentations have failed simply because salespeople didn't want to "offend" the potential customer and didn't explain the purpose of their visit from the very beginning? Otherwise, you may have several "good" meetings that eventually go nowhere, leaving both the potential customer and the salesperson unsure of the next steps.

Unfortunately, we don't live in a perfect world but rather in a complex one, with complicated people and behaviors that are often unpredictable. You might find yourself in a situation where the person you're speaking with says something like:

"Hold on. I haven't decided yet. You're moving too fast for me."

What do you do in such a situation?

This information is certainly valuable because you need to know where there are still unresolved issues. If you don't know the problem, you can't successfully do your job. It's always better to identify the issue early on through a systematic approach of "progressive information gathering" than to wait until the last moment and realize, just when you want to close the deal, that you haven't paid attention to some crucial detail.

Gather the information you need to move forward in the sales cycle, even if it's not what you want to hear.

By collecting information and feedback from the potential customer, you can address issues that haven't yet been explicitly mentioned. You might discover that, even though you entered the meeting expecting to sell product A and the customer showed considerable interest in it, the questions raised during the conversation reveal that the customer can only achieve their goals with product B. Your job is to solve problems, not to force the customer into your ideas. Therefore, it's better to shift focus to product B. You can only reach this important conclusion if you pay close attention to the feedback from your conversation partner.

Let me emphasize one more thing: sales cycles vary across different industries. Simply put, you will never know in advance whether a potential buyer will ultimately make a purchasing decision or not. You'll need to have enough patience to navigate your way slowly and steadily. Understand that you can't do this until both you and your conversation partner know how far they've come and what direction they're actually heading in.

You Engage the Potential Customer.

Engaging a potential customer is actually a complex task that can be hard to define. Perhaps it's easier to explain what engagement is not. Engaging the customer is certainly not about reacting immediately or reflexively to every comment or critical remark.

Take a look at the following conversation:

Potential Customer:
"When we last talked about these things, I'll never forget our first meetings."

You:
"That's fine, we can work on Mondays. That day is just like any other for me."

Potential Customer:
"I actually meant something different—because we met on a Monday morning, we weren't as busy as we should have been."

You:
"I understand your concern. We can meet whenever you prefer, and we can cancel our Monday morning meetings."

This kind of conversation isn't meaningful for either party—it's just a form of ping-pong dialogue. Engaging the customer means responding clearly and unambiguously to both their explicitly stated and implied needs, provided you understand them, even if not all are directly related to the product or service you offer. Only by doing this can you establish a mutual understanding and framework for addressing important issues with the potential customer.

You'll need to find the best way to build these relationships, considering the unique dynamics of the customer's age, position, personality, and even race compared to your own. It's pointless to disregard these differences, and ignoring them in your sales activities is self-defeating.

Unique Characteristics of a Potential Customer.

Every potential customer is unique, each reacting differently to your words. Some may feel like they have all the time in the world, while others may consider even a fifteen-minute meeting too long. Some have succeeded in life because they were somewhat unreliable, while others relied on courage and trust to build their careers in business.

What's important is that respect cannot be earned through a single, one-size-fits-all "recipe" aimed at making the first few minutes of a meeting with a potential client as successful as possible. First, you must figure out what is particularly important to each potential customer, and then carefully consider how you can meet their expectations.

Here are some tips on how to choose a potential customer and start a productive initial conversation. Of course, you will also need to adapt to each individual situation. Discuss topics you are familiar with and feel comfortable talking about. Don't engage in abstract discussions about expressionism in art if you don't know enough about the subject. Instead, talk about electric railways, Walt Disney, or how to memorize important information more easily, if these things are closer to you and you know more about them. A topic you are familiar with, and that is somehow related to your conversation partner, will surely make a good impression.

Remember that it is in your best interest to start the conversation by focusing on your own observations and experiences, naturally and tactfully. This way, you reduce the pressure on your interlocutor, who may have expected you to try to push a sale in front of a witness.

Also, talk about your surroundings. The office you're sitting in is a reflection of its owner's personality. With a little effort, you can find something that serves as a positive starting point for discussing how your conversation partner has organized their workspace.

Help Your Conversation Partner in Subtle Ways.

When your conversation partner begins to talk about themselves, show genuine interest. In such cases, I usually put down my pen, which I use for taking notes. This response is an unspoken acknowledgment that their experiences are highly interesting and educational for you. It's always beneficial to get your conversation partner to talk about their own experiences. People who talk about themselves are more relaxed than those who avoid such conversations.

Show sincere interest and never forget that you are there to help. If your conversation partner shares their problems, treat them with as much attention and care as if they were your own. After all, you want to be the one who helps them solve those problems, not one of your competitors.

You Identify Key Requirements

Is it worth setting a goal to "find customers who need your product"? All the time? The answer to this question is more complex than you might think.

The short news: the market has changed, and if you want to succeed, you'll need to change as well.

Most of those selling today are not creating new markets. Often, we don't follow the commonly mentioned formula of "find a need and meet it," because it's not as simple as it seems at first glance. For almost half a century, our market economy has satisfied the basic needs of consumers at a scale and level of success never before experienced in history. In this regard, the market hasn't completely succeeded yet, but it has advanced enough to change the way sellers operate. If sellers want to succeed these days, they need to identify the unmet needs that can be fulfilled for a savvy and spoiled consumer base, which is more aware than ever that when it comes to new products or services, the choice is theirs.

We already have plenty of cars, for instance, and copiers. We also have many options for health insurance. If your job is to sell a car, a copier, or health insurance, you'll have to include something new and particularly appealing in your offer, tailored to the specific customer. Today's customers are increasingly knowledgeable, and it's more likely than ever that they already have some experience with the product or service you are offering. You will need to adjust your approach as much as possible to meet the specific demands of the target group of potential buyers. Failing to do so could result in significant problems.

Find a Potential Customer Who Fits Your Idea of a Satisfied Client

I don't mean to suggest that there are no buyers purchasing a car for the first time, or companies seeking additional health insurance for the first time. The number of "new" customers varies by geographic region and economic sector. However, an important fact is that most good salespeople I meet don't focus much on first-time buyers of a product or service. Their main goal is typically not to discover a need for their product but to find a customer whose needs they can meet better than anyone else.

Find your market segment, your area of expertise. In short, where you have the best chance of success. You can learn a lot by understanding the challenges faced by different types of "educated" clients whom you know you can serve. Only then do you seek new prospects, aiming to convert them into loyal clients. The most successful salespeople I know have developed a particular sense of which potential customers they have the best chance with, and they approach as many people as possible.

For a person who has been satisfied with product X for twenty years, your priority is not to broadly investigate their general needs, but rather to focus on identifying the needs that can be met by product Y, which you are offering. Does the potential customer need better service? More flexible payment options? A lower price? More frequent contact with the seller? There are thousands of variations. It's often difficult to identify the right needs, perhaps because even the potential buyer hasn't fully defined them. This is where you step in to assist.

The Salesperson as an Attentive Teacher, Not a Bulldozer

In some areas of sales, your primary focus will be on people who are first-time buyers, such as those interested in purchasing insurance. It would be overly simplistic to say it's just about finding their needs. Any good insurance agent will tell you that their job is primarily about educating, filling the knowledge gaps of someone who is interested in insurance for the first time, and providing the necessary information for the person to make an informed decision about the right type of coverage. This process requires a lot of tact, patience, and persistence—much time after identifying the correct needs.

Now, think about this: what if you're dealing with someone who already knows they need life insurance and doesn't require any help or new information to sign a policy? They simply call the insurance company. But if you are dealing with a person who is already using a competing product or service, which is often the case, you must remember that the need has already been identified to some extent. In fact, this person has invested considerable time in their current product, even though they might be too busy to fully engage with you. More sales deals have failed than you can imagine simply because the salesperson didn't realize that for an "educated" buyer, the focus should primarily be on identifying and addressing new needs that their current product or service cannot meet.

The Importance of Perspective and Patience

Keep things in perspective. There's nothing stopping you from talking about your product openly. The real question is how you approach it. It's pointless to dwell on how great it is to have product Y, which you're offering, compared to having nothing at all. However, if you discuss the clear advantages of product Y over competing product X, your chances of success are much higher. Consider every potential customer as part of an evolving sales relationship, understanding that each interaction takes time to develop. Patience is key to nurturing these relationships and guiding them toward success.

win to win

**Count to Three Before Surrendering to Triumph.
It's a Dream.**

You're at work, thinking about your tasks, when the phone rings, and someone unexpectedly offers you a deal. Amazing, right? I know these temptations well. After all, you're eager to make a sale. Life is complicated enough—you've spent the whole day planning and negotiating, and here comes a sale you feel you've long deserved. Naturally, you'd do anything not to lose this sudden opportunity. That's why you might jump in without thinking.
But it's better not to.
This takes some discipline. Let's be honest—it takes a lot of discipline. But if you truly want to seize this unexpected phone opportunity, believe me, it's best to first take a deep breath, count to three, and follow these simple steps.

Rules to Follow:

First Time: Before establishing any business relationship, consider whether this is someone you've never interacted with before, and therefore, you don't know what approach will suit them best. You could easily go down the wrong path. Start by exchanging a few polite, general remarks and try to gauge what kind of person you're dealing with.

Second Time: Find out what's really happening. For example, say: "I'm really glad we connected. Could you tell me what prompted you to reach out to me?" It's crucial to know exactly who you're dealing with, because without clarity, no sale is possible. Things might not be as they appear at first glance. Sometimes people call, and it seems like they're ready to sign a contract, but in reality, much more persuasion is needed. Try to gather as much information as possible about the person you'll be doing business with, and resist the temptation to jump into selling right away. Don't rush.

Third Time: Suggest an in-person meeting, even if your contact wants to finalize the deal over the phone—unless, of course, you specialize in phone sales. Personal contact is key to building a stronger relationship.

Don't harbor any illusions that sales are easy or guaranteed. Selling is a numbers game: your job is to turn the odds in your favor in as many ways and in as many situations as possible.

If you follow these guidelines consistently over time, your success is assured.

Do you know how to rebrand your product or service?

How can you adapt an existing product or service so that it best meets the needs of a potential customer?

In my lectures, I often talk about "flexibility," referring to the interchangeability of various products and services. Dentists use both gold and silver for dental fillings due to the mutual interchangeability of the two precious metals, which can perform the same task. Similarly, you can think about your product or service and how you can adjust it to also serve new clients and their specific needs well.

Paper Clips:

Let's look at a simple example. Suppose you sell paper clips. Have you ever thought about how differently people use them? Of course, we primarily think of these clips as small metal objects typically used to bind individual sheets of paper, but some people unbend them to clean tight corners of office furniture, others use them to repair broken glasses, and some use them to assemble egg chains. I myself have successfully used these clips several times, and certainly with due caution, to remove a floppy disk that refused to eject from my computer.

Beyond the main function of paper clips, there are dozens of other possible uses. Can your product or service be used in hundreds of different ways you hadn't thought of before? Before answering "no," consider that you don't need hundreds of additional uses to increase sales. Sometimes, one is enough.

Baking powder is intended for making cakes, right? That's true, but some people emphasize the excellent usefulness of baking powder for deodorizing the inside of a refrigerator. Do you know anyone who uses baking powder for this purpose?

That's why, in such cases, I talk about adaptability.

Ask yourself:

Does what you sell serve only one purpose? Can you help adapt your product or service for other uses? Can you enhance your product with a new feature so that it serves an additional purpose? Can you introduce it to different groups of potential buyers?

A lot depends on how well you can seek out new opportunities and adapt to them. I don't mean that you must become the next Henry Ford or Thomas Alva Edison at all costs if you want to expand your product's usefulness. Start as simply as possible, by offering just one additional version. If you manage to find new opportunities in this way, you can accelerate your career or even change your field of activity!

Imagine that you are a consultant (which, in fact, you are!).

———— •❖• — •❖• ————

Treat your sales efforts as a consulting assignment. Many years ago, I found myself at a dead end while working with a potential buyer. I wanted to develop a special program for him, but things didn't go as I had hoped.

So, I finally said to the potential buyer: "Charlie, instead of continuing our search, I'm asking you to give me some time to think about our goals, and I'll come back next week with new ideas. If you like the new ideas, we can continue our conversation."

He agreed, and in the end, I sold him my program. Shortly after that meeting, I realized what I had actually done. I had chosen the same approach that I would have used with a potential buyer who would only want and expect an analysis of the problems their company's salespeople were facing.

For a moment, I set aside the burden of making a sale and considered that I couldn't offer the potential buyer the right solution because I hadn't fully studied and assessed his problems yet. The effectiveness of this trick lies in the fact that you momentarily place yourself in the role of a consultant, stop, and look at the situation from a different perspective.

Problem Solving.

The best salespeople are also the best problem solvers. If you sell cars, you must put yourself in the shoes of someone solving transportation problems. If you sell copiers, you need to take on the role of someone solving photocopying problems. And if you sell mobile phones, you also need to focus on solving communication issues. But you must first thoroughly understand these problems before trying to solve them.

For many salespeople, the advisory principle can be simplified even further. If you are selling another company's products, you need to see yourself as someone solving financial profitability problems. This is the key task they will ultimately assign to you: how you can help increase profit. Everything you do, everything you offer, must ultimately lead to your potential client's company operating with higher profitability. Align your goals and approach with this key requirement, and everything will be fine—this is an important step toward success in sales.

If you're not willing to genuinely help people solve their problems, I'll tell you that, unfortunately, you've chosen the wrong profession as a salesperson. If you can't focus all your efforts on helping others achieve their important goals, you'll either base your sales on manipulation or fail to convince potential buyers that you're offering them something valuable. Both paths lead to constant rejection and failure. Of course, you want to avoid this at all costs.

One dictionary defines the word "counsel" as "seeking advice, information, or guidance from someone." In my view, this explanation perfectly describes the relationship between a well-informed potential buyer and a professional salesperson. As a salesperson, you should advise your client on how you can help them solve their problems. You should provide them with all the information necessary to address those problems, and you should guide them properly so that your business relationship is as effective, harmonious, and mutually successful as possible.

So work as a consultant... because that's exactly what you are!

You make an offer at the first meeting.

This is probably the easiest piece of advice to follow from all the tips I've gathered in this book, but most salespeople prefer to overlook it. Some are even afraid of it, even though they know perfectly well that it works wonders for others.

A young salesperson once told me: "Steve, I'm not in my office, I'm in the office of a potential client who's shown interest by inviting me. They'll have to invite me again if they want further contact. 'I'm a guest.'"

Nonsense!

First of all, as a salesperson, you made the first contact and made it clear from the very beginning that your goal is to help the potential buyer. You've shown that your primary interest is in solving their problem. So why not offer the potential client a follow-up meeting where you can show them more specifically what solution you're preparing for them?

To me, at least, this argument is so convincing that no further explanation is needed.

But I'm always surprised to see how astonished salespeople are by this suggestion. Here are a few concrete responses I've received from salespeople when I suggested they offer a follow-up meeting during the first visit:

"I can't offer the next meeting because I don't know when I'll be back in the area."

"I can't offer a follow-up meeting because I don't yet know how long it will take to prepare the proposal."

"I can't offer the next meeting because I don't have the pricing ready."

"I don't dare suggest another meeting because I'm afraid the potential buyer won't accept it."

These are honest statements from many salespeople. Can you believe them?

If you need to estimate roughly how long it will take to prepare your proposal or negotiate prices with a colleague, then assess it as realistically as possible! The worst that could happen is that you'll need to ask the potential client to reschedule the proposed meeting.

Your Goal.

You didn't schedule the first meeting by accident or out of mere courtesy, but because you had an important goal: to help the potential client solve their problems with your product or service. Even at the end of your first meeting, you're still pursuing that same goal, which is why it's appropriate and completely understandable to suggest continuing the conversation and scheduling a follow-up meeting.

Unless, of course, you receive a decisively dismissive "no" at the first meeting, the conversation must continue, and further meetings are necessary. The best time to plan the next meeting is during the first one. Both you and your client likely have a calendar on hand, so it's inexcusable to leave without knowing when you'll meet again.

"Alright, Mr. Jones. I think we've accomplished everything we could today. I'd like to meet with you again in a couple of weeks to show you what we can do for your company. How about Friday the 15th?"

Pay close attention to their response, because you'll get one, and make sure you're well-prepared for the next meeting.

Taking Notes.

Taking notes during a meeting with a potential client can become one of the most effective sales tools.

Focus on Solutions.

Writing down important details will further reinforce your purpose for both you and your conversation partner. It shows that you're there to learn as much as possible about their problems.

Listening.

By taking notes, you'll be able to listen more attentively. With a blank sheet of paper in front of you, you tend to focus even more on each word, ensuring that no important detail is missed.

Authority and Power.

Taking notes will help you gain authority and control. Believe me, it's during the first twenty minutes of most initial meetings that you establish the greatest authority.

Analytical Skills.

Note-taking also strengthens your analytical abilities. When you take notes during a meeting, you're engaging three senses at once: writing (your hand when you write), hearing (as you listen to the speaker), and sight (as you look at what you've written). In my experience, a person is in a much better position to find the most suitable solution when they approach the problem with all three senses: typing, hearing, and sight.

Extracting as Much Information as Possible.

By taking notes, you encourage the speaker to open up more and provide you with more information. In every lecture, I receive further confirmation of my point about the importance of note-taking for developing communication. When I just stand in front of an audience and ask them, "What was good about the presentation you just heard?" usually nothing happens. But if I write on the board "GOOD PRESENTATION QUALITIES" and then ask for comments, the answers come pouring in!

Positive Signals.

Writing sends strong positive signals to the potential client, and there aren't that many such useful signs. For example, if your conversation partner says they have 500 trucks, each capable of carrying 75 of your products, and that they run 320 days a year, and they see you writing down: "500 x 75 x 320 days a year," they'll be pleased to know that you're interested and paying attention.

Some Suggestions.

I recommend using a regular notebook with a hard cardboard cover, sturdy enough to write on your lap if necessary. Your notes should be legible and not too lengthy. Always keep in mind that they should be understandable to both you and your conversation partner.

If needed, include large enough diagrams in your notes to further emphasize what's written, and show these diagrams to your conversation partner.

You Prepare a Plan with Every New Potential Client.

Every time I met a new potential client, I would tell myself: "This is something new, a person I've never dealt with before. What am I going to do to treat this person a little differently?"

It may all seem like a routine repetition to you, but your conversation partner has never worked with you in the sales process before. One of the best ways I know to avoid feeling like it's just another repetition of the usual process (even the best salespeople sometimes can't help but feel this way) is to prepare a written plan specifically designed for the new potential client. The notes from your first and subsequent meetings will serve as a valuable foundation for this plan.

"Oh, it's the same again!"

After a while, you become more familiar with certain objections and issues, and there's nothing easier than carelessly lumping the person you're speaking with into a box and saying: "I already know this issue. It's the same as the guy from ABC company." Well, yes and no. The problem is not the same as ABC because the person who just mentioned it has absolutely no connection to ABC. The potential client who raises an objection does so in good faith. I admit, this statement may sound a bit odd, but it's true. When your conversation partner takes the time to talk to you about their problems, they are providing you with important information as well as key data for necessary changes to your product or service. Listening is the first part of the secret, and finding mutually acceptable solutions is the second part.

Understand what these problems are, while being mindful of the unique circumstances and conditions that characterize your conversation partner. Then, write down possible solutions and, together with your partner, draft a plan that best suits the situation.

Doctor, Doctor...

If you go to the doctor because you have a stomachache, you don't care that in his long career, he has already dealt with three thousand patients with stomach pain before you. The last thing you expect from such an experienced doctor is for him to rush into the office, perform a quick check, mutter some Latin words you've never heard before, write something on a prescription, and then dash off. No. You expect him to ask you how you're feeling, how long you've had the pain, where it hurts exactly, if you're allergic to any medications, and other such questions. If the doctor patiently asks you all the questions you expect, you're likely to be a better patient, and it will be easier for you to decide to visit this doctor again in the future.

You are also a kind of doctor. It doesn't matter how many patients you've dealt with before. The patient in front of you is the only and most important one for you at this moment. Like the best doctors, you need to do everything possible to give the patient the most accurate diagnosis and provide the most effective treatment. Only by acting this way will you improve the atmosphere for your work and thus increase the likelihood that your patient will have a positive attitude toward you, which is, in fact, the foundation for many dramatic recoveries!

Ask for Recommendations

My favorite story about recommendations is related to Bill, a highly successful salesman whom I know well. Every year, he spends his vacation in some exotic location, like Fiji, the Cayman Islands, or Hawaii. Often, these holidays are a reward for his sales achievements. Once a year, Bill informs his clients and potential customers about his return from paradise, where he spent his prize vacation. The purpose of this letter is to thank the clients for their cooperation, while at the same time emphasizing that as a salesman, he only achieved his goal by successfully helping his clients achieve theirs. Nice, isn't it?

At the end of this letter, there is a paragraph that goes something like this:

"As you know, success in my business depends on recommendations. I would be very grateful if you could take a moment to write down the names and phone numbers of three or four businesspeople in your area who you think might benefit from talking to me. If you prefer that I do not mention you when contacting them, please note that in the field I've provided. Let me once again sincerely thank you. I appreciate your cooperation, which has been extremely valuable to me and, I hope, to you as well."

Some may call me naive, but I firmly believe that there is a direct cause-and-effect relationship between well-crafted letters like the one I mentioned and Bill's enviable vacations to exotic places, as well as the numerous sales awards this man has received throughout his career.

The numbers speak for themselves.

Let's play a multiplication game. Suppose each of five people gives you five recommendations, which totals twenty-five. Now, let's assume that out of these new referrals, sixty percent of the people give you new recommendations. That's fifteen times five, or seventy-five new potential clients. Let's continue: if sixty percent of those seventy-five businesspeople give you five new recommendations... you can imagine the outcome. If you've decided to expand your client base exponentially (and why not?), you'll find it hard to beat asking for recommendations as a starting point.

Recommendations serve as an excellent foundation for a successful sales career, yet salespeople often hesitate to ask for them. Typically, they fear that by asking a business partner for the contacts of friends or acquaintances who might benefit from their product, they may jeopardize their established business relationships.

Follow your instincts.

You should be able to determine without much difficulty whether you have a satisfied client or not, and whether your potential client is excited about your offer or not. If you can easily figure this out, it means you've built the foundation for a productive and mutually beneficial business relationship. Why wouldn't one of your clients share their experience of such a partnership with their business friends? Assuming there are no competing companies or other conflicts of interest, you can definitely expect businesspeople to gladly, perhaps even enthusiastically, provide the recommendations you've asked for.

And how can you make good use of the references you gather? Suppose you aim to attract five new potential clients in one week. Always carry a stack of 3 x 5-inch index cards with you, and after meeting with a client or a prospect, simply say something like: "Mr. Jones, I'm sure there are a few businesspeople in your industry or geographic region who could benefit from a personal discussion about the product I'm offering."

When you say this, show Jones five blank cards and ask: "Do you know five such people I could talk to?" You're actually helping Mr. Jones by laying out the five cards, making your request clear and very specific. Your professional approach and the trust Mr. Jones has in you ensure that your request won't come across as rude or inappropriate.

Laying the cards on the table one by one, you first write only the names, then ask about business connections, addresses, and other details that may interest you. You're doing this mainly because you want to make the first, and most important, part of the job—identifying the people you want to talk to—as simple as possible.

A Direct Approach.

I know a salesman who, in this situation, would probably ask his customer: "Frank, would it be wrong for you to call these people instead of me?" Of course, Frank would nod and suggest the salesman call them himself. Then the salesman would say: "You're right, it's better if I call them myself. I hope you don't mind if I mention your name?" He never received two "no's" in a row, and he especially wanted a "yes" to the second question.

This might be called an aggressive approach, and I wouldn't recommend it to all of you. In any case, the example clearly illustrates the point that you can achieve a lot if you take the initiative and ask for what you need directly, without any roundabout ways.

You are showing enthusiasm.

When I suggest that you demonstrate enthusiasm, I don't mean that you should hug a potential customer, shake their hand ten times with all your might, or give endless compliments about their appearance. Fortunately, there is a significant difference between excitement and poorly concealed panic. Excitement builds bridges, while panic destroys them.

A sales meeting, like any other meeting, is characterized by interaction. First of all, it takes some time to take off. If you understand the internal dynamics at play when you first contact a potential customer, you will realize that enthusiasm needs to be present as you continue to engage.

The Early Period.

When meeting a new person, we go through various phases. Firstly, there is the introductory phase of getting to know each other, which is a kind of exploration. During this phase, you cannot convincingly communicate everything you want to say about solving the potential customer's problem, because you don't know each other well enough yet. Your counterpart, like most adults, will require a certain "trial" period before they are ready to establish a more friendly rapport with you. Therefore, in the very early stages of the meeting, it is advisable to exercise restraint in showing enthusiasm. A trusting demeanor, good eye contact (but not so intense that it feels like staring), a firm handshake, and a relaxed posture are all ways to express your excitement about the new business relationship you intend to cultivate.

Later Stage

Only you can tell when a potential customer has entered the second stage of friendly contact, but rest assured, this change will be noticeable. This stage is characterized by a more relaxed and open approach, often reflected in a less restrained body language. You'll know it's happening when the potential customer listens to you attentively not just because they agreed to, but because they genuinely want to. Once you notice this important shift—which could happen during the first meeting or any of the subsequent ones—you can adjust the "grammar" of your approach.

You might decide to use your hands more for gesturing or adopt the style your client prefers. You can also start using less formal phrases, such as: "Take a look for yourself," "What do you think about this?" or "Let me tell you what we've done."

Try to avoid repetitive mechanical gestures or responses, as such repetitions make the meeting feel unspontaneous, dampening any expected enthusiasm. How would you feel if your conversation partner kept nodding up and down, disregarding what you had to say?

Keeping Eyes Open

These are general guidelines. Your individual interactions with potential clients will, of course, vary, just as clients differ from one another. However, it's worth emphasizing that a certain level of enthusiasm on your part—especially during the second and later visits—can be a significant advantage for a successful sale.

Giving Yourself Due Credit.

Talk about yourself, but remain humble. These two instructions are not mutually exclusive, though they may seem so at first glance. I want to teach you how to do both at the same time. There's nothing wrong with going into a potential client's office and enthusiastically, proudly talking about what you do. Far too many salespeople fail to realize that this is exactly why they enter the market in the first place. The only danger is overstepping. Fortunately, avoiding an arrogant approach is relatively easy.

Balanced Confidence.

When you walk in the door and greet a potential client, you want to convey a sense of success, confidence, and flexibility—without making declarations. This is proof of professionalism, something you can rightly take pride in. You need to be able to discuss things in detail, and thanks to this opportunity, you've achieved it.

I'm not suggesting you brag to a prospective buyer about your wonderful kids, your golf skills, or how much money you make. That's a game you simply can't win, no matter how the conversation ends. Instead, I recommend confidently emphasizing your ability to succeed at your chosen task, but even here, you must exercise considerable discretion. You need to develop a good sense of judgment to know when to step back. Also, recognize that what works perfectly for Person A in a given situation may have a completely different, even adverse, effect with Person B in another context.

Still, keep in mind that there is also a risk that, by not reading certain signs correctly, you might achieve the opposite effect. However, the fact is that many salespeople make too little of an impression on prospective clients, and that's a problem too. In my view, at least you won't drown in the anonymous crowd of mediocre salespeople that clients often have to put up with nearly every day.

Praise Yourself.

What I recommend does carry some risk, but I believe the risk is well worth it. Try the next possible approach with a client you meet, something like this:

"Mr. Jones, it's a pleasure to see you. I've had a busy week—we just successfully completed Project XYZ. Let me tell you a few words about this important achievement."

Now, here is a person who can confidently talk about significant accomplishments, a quick-minded conversation partner. In an earlier chapter, I used the analogy of a doctor and a patient. This time, I'll use this comparison in a slightly different way.

Imagine you walk into a doctor's office, and as soon as he enters, you realize he looks even worse than you do. He's coughing and sneezing, holding a half-burnt cigarette in shaky fingers. He's sluggish and struggles to focus on your concerns. Is this the person who's supposed to resolve your health issues? For many professionals, there are two types of people: those who add value to everything they do and those who diminish everything they touch. Prove that you belong to the first group. Show your value as vividly and convincingly as possible. Be boldly proud!

If you can do all this without giving an air of superiority or excessive boasting, your self-praise will be seen as a guarantee of security and reliability. They will see you not as an arrogant braggart but as someone who rightfully takes pride in their accomplishments and confidently believes in their ability to deliver on the task at hand.

You're Speaking the Truth.
(It's easier to remember this way.)

When determining the amount of "white lies" in conversation, polite remarks like, "I'm glad you came," were also considered—even when someone might not actually feel that way. When I recommend that you tell the truth to your clients, I don't mean the harmless social lies we often accept as part of polite conventions.

Building Bridges.

Salespeople are relationship-oriented, basing their connections on trust and personal contact, and they often rely heavily on the strength of these business ties. These facts might make a case for the occasional "white lie" to smooth things over, and such lies are by no means the worst kind. Let's look at a few examples.

"Wow, what a beautiful office! I'd love to work in such a pleasant space." (In reality, the office where you work alone is far nicer.)

This is fine. For some salespeople, it's easier to establish rapport with a potential client by paying them a compliment to break the ice. What if this involves a little exaggeration, as in this case? Even if the potential client later finds out you actually work in a much better office than theirs, don't worry too much about your flattery —as long as it was delivered tactfully.

"As for the delivery date you're asking about, I don't foresee any issues with that, though I'll need to confirm a few details with our technical team after we wrap up formalities today." (In reality, you know very well that you'll miss the requested delivery date by two weeks, regardless of what you tell the production team.)

Red Alert! Here, you're trying to establish a new business relationship with a potential client, yet you're deliberately presenting your capabilities in a skewed way to reassure them. If things go wrong later (and this is likely), your client will not remember your partial excuse about needing to check the delivery date; they'll remember your promise to deliver by the first of the month, not the fifteenth. At this point, the client will see you not as someone who solves problems but as the cause of their problems. They'll view you as an unreliable seller who overpromises. On this basis, they'll probably be reluctant to entrust you with any future business.

A Slippery Slope.

If you're still not convinced, consider this: once you get used to telling everyone what they want to hear, you're likely to run into serious trouble. You'll end up working with fifteen different clients, to whom you've made fifteen different promises, none of which have a real basis or can actually be fulfilled. It's only a matter of time before you become hopelessly entangled and completely incapacitated.

Don't risk letting something like this happen to you. Instead, choose to tell the truth—it's much easier to remember.

You're Selling Yourself to Yourself.

Below, I've compiled a few ideas you can use to motivate yourself. Take advantage of them!

Avoid Listening to the Radio During Your Morning Commute.

Morning radio shows are often filled with discouraging news that you can't change anyway. You'll hear all the bad news soon enough, so save your morning for more stimulating activities. Instead, get a few motivational tapes to listen to on the way to work, or use the time to go over your plans for the day. I know one salesperson who took this advice so seriously that he doesn't even know if his car radio still works.

Be Specific in Your Goals, and Also in Your Rewards.

Maybe you dream of a Lamborghini. Place a picture of that sports car on your desk or your refrigerator at home. Or perhaps you have a more realistic goal in mind: to close six sales contracts next month. Write down your goal on a piece of paper. This makes it more tangible and increases the likelihood that you'll reach it within your set timeframe.

Get Support.

I'm amazed by the number of successful team sales I see around me. Usually, it's two people selling completely independently but regularly helping each other along the way. We all need advice and constructive criticism. For most of us, this is far better than working entirely alone. If you can create this type of cooperation in your work environment, give it a try and see if it works.

Take a Walk.
It's true that you need a break at noon, and I don't recommend working through it every day. My research on midday breaks among salespeople has strengthened my belief that those who take a one-hour break and go for a walk are more productive and actually have better sales results than their peers who don't allow themselves even an hour of rest.

Leave Yourself Encouraging Messages.
"I can absolutely do this," "Most of the things I fear will never happen," "I've successfully solved issues for 500 clients." Leave a note on your desk with a similar motivating message.

See Things from the Right Perspective.
In my office, we have a habit of sending each other funny messages, like "It's not brain surgery!" Usually, it really isn't that serious. Missed calls, forgotten deadlines, persistent client issues... all of these can be complex and sometimes even awkward, but it's not the end of the world. Often, problems seem harder to solve at first glance than they actually are, and it helps to keep that in mind throughout the workday. For me, this is especially important between two and four in the afternoon, when the workday really starts to feel like an endless series of brain surgeries. Is something similar happening to you right now? If so, that's the time to take a proper break.

"The Early Bird Catches the Worm."

The Early Hour is the Golden Hour.

Did you know you can avoid the "secretary trap" by making important phone calls before nine a.m.? Many decision-makers are in their offices before most of their staff arrives, so there's a good chance they'll answer your call personally.

An Early Start Has Several Benefits.

Above, I mentioned one clear advantage of starting your workday early, but there are many others. For one thing, you'll better manage the "crisis atmosphere" that hits offices around nine a.m., and for another, you'll gain time to relax a bit and get organized outside the typical rush of the workday. These are important advantages, especially during demanding times.

The Commute.

I suspect your morning commute will be much easier if you leave home a bit earlier. This may seem like a small benefit until you realize how significant your mood is to your sales performance. Nowadays, in big cities, you can easily spend an hour or more just moving from point A to point B in traffic. It's a big waste of precious time and, even worse, can ruin your mood, which is often unavoidable.

So, if you spend the first sixty or more minutes of your morning cursing at fellow drivers or getting annoyed with stoplights, don't be surprised if you lack a friendly tone during your first calls of the day. You'll lose some of your usual dedication to your work before you've even spoken to a single potential client, which is, of course, an irreparable loss. Having enough time for yourself means you're in better shape when you work with others.

Finally, let me add an important thought based on my experience and the experience of many successful salespeople I've worked with: you'll find your day to be much more productive if you set aside a few minutes of "quiet time" for yourself before the panic and time crunches begin.

Ideally, we would arrive at work early enough to have some alone time and then make a few calls to colleagues—mainly to warm up—so that our first calls of the day don't go to potential buyers.

You Read Professional Publications.
(From Your Territory and Your Clients' Industry.)

How many people do you think read a trade newsletter like American Road Engineer? Or the respected newsletter Publishers Weekly? How about those subscribed to a professional weekly like This Week or magazines like Billboard or Variety?

You won't find these specialized professional newsletters in most newsstands, but the aforementioned publications and countless others might be some of the most valuable resources you can get your hands on. The industry your clients operate in likely has its own newsletters, followed by everyone interested in that field. By familiarizing yourself with these, you can gain a distinct advantage over many of your sales competitors. You'll gain insights into industry trends, and more importantly, better understand the business environment your clients face. While a subscription to these professional journals may not be inexpensive, a little effort might yield a few back issues at larger bookstores or libraries.

Your Decisive Advantage: Information.

You'll soon find that your understanding of the technical "Latvian language" used by your target audience improves significantly after reading a few articles from industry journals dedicated to that field. Admittedly, some of the articles may be tough reading, especially those aimed at a more demanding audience. However, you'll feel much more comfortable when you can at least approximate the meaning of those technical terms you previously just nodded along to.

Additionally, these professional publications often contain sections like "Who's Who" or "What's Happening," which can be incredibly useful sources of information. Here, you'll find names of companies and branches, as well as names of individuals recently hired or promoted. Who wouldn't be flattered by a short congratulatory note, followed by a call from you a few days later to discuss a product or service that may be of interest?

You Stay Up-to-Date with All the News.

You might even decide to cut out the most interesting articles from the professional journals. This archive can be invaluable, especially when you want to break the ice with a new prospect. For me, I'd much prefer to share three interesting industry-specific insights from a trade journal with a contact rather than spend twenty minutes discussing the weather or their lovely children.

Emphasizing the Importance of Your Visit the Next Day.

Make sure to call or write to a prospective client the day after your visit. Most salespeople, despite their intentions, often overlook this essential follow-up step. I highly recommend making these valuable follow-up contacts a regular part of your workday schedule. Aim to reach out no later than the day after your visit to the potential client. The primary goal of this "support measure" is to reaffirm your presence and reassure the prospect of your commitment to addressing their needs. Remember to approach this with the right amount of tact and keep your message concise.

A Phone Call Is Enough.

"Mr. Smith, this is Maude Powers, a sales representative from InfoMira. I'll only take a minute of your time, as I wanted to thank you for meeting with me yesterday, especially given your busy schedule. I found our meeting extremely valuable. What do you think?"

I suggest a phone call initially because it's one of the simplest ways to convey such a message in today's business world. However, I'd like to add that a letter on your company's stationery, though considered old-fashioned by some, can attract remarkably positive attention from the recipient. Time constraints and the general reluctance among many businesspeople to write letters may deter you from choosing this approach, but I stress that a well-crafted, courteously written letter can have a surprisingly impactful effect. Keep the letter brief and to the point to avoid spending too much time on it.

Remember.

Growth begins where accusations stop.

Engaging Businesspeople and Community Groups.

⬅➡

Public speaking is one of those activities people often approach with great fear. However, I suggest you work on developing your speaking skills and sharing your expertise with audiences beyond your own industry. Believe that you can also speak effectively to others.

Speaking as an Expert.

This is truly a double-edged sword. On one hand, you can gain more confidence because people see you as an expert in your field. But on the other hand, if you don't feel like an expert, don't try to create that impression. Your clients undoubtedly rely on your knowledge and experience. Consider the fact that you are already familiar with your field and discuss sales daily. Only you can judge what further steps are needed to become a speaker and make sure you get noticed. After all, you deserve it.

The first advantage you gain from public speaking is validation of your efforts. You already know internally that you and your company are capable of handling tasks A, B, and C, but you'll also convince others of this if you step onto a stage and talk to an audience about these challenges. If you're unsure whether such a statement will positively impact your work with potential clients, then perhaps you need more experience in the sales field.

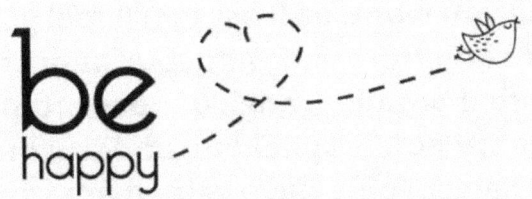

The second advantage is even more important. Research has shown that after presentations by salespeople and sales consultants, an average of ten listeners want to learn more about the speakers' products and services. In fact, this means that one-tenth of your audience will become your new potential clients. Who knows what might happen if you take the initiative to hand out business cards during breaks and especially after classes? You will definitely have to put in quite a bit of effort to prepare before you feel relaxed enough to speak in front of a large group of people, but I assure you that the effort is worth it. Don't forget that even the most experienced professional instructors complain about stage fright. It won't be any different for you, but make the adrenaline work for you. Where should a salesperson give a speech? Everywhere and at any opportunity to speak in front of an audience.

Also, consider scheduling an appointment with the Chamber of Commerce to participate in a local roundtable. Speaking to members of various clubs or community groups related to your business is also welcomed.

Get to work!

Join a club or any organization of your choice, express your desire, and you'll see how things unfold. It is quite likely that they will gladly accept your initiative to speak before a wider audience. Ask yourself, what do you have to lose? Absolutely nothing! Even if your speech doesn't go exactly as you want, at least you'll feel good knowing you made an effort and that your name has been introduced to a broader range of new potential clients.

Be sure to try public speaking, and trust me, many successful salespeople have gained amazing benefits from their presentations.

When the opportunity arises, you pass on your experience to others.
Offer your help.
Why should someone help someone else if you don't need it, especially if you find it impossible that you will ever need this person's help in return? I admit that answering this question is not so simple. Perhaps an example from the world of sports can help. I have often been amazed to see players from opposing teams sharing good advice with each other here and there during a match. In fact, these are not strategically important insights that would give the opponent a decisive advantage if shared unnecessarily, but usually comments that are equally important for players on both teams, such as about technical flaws on the field. Players on opposing teams do not exchange these well-meaning comments because they do not see each other as adversaries—they do not forget this—but because they consider each other colleagues. After all, it's nice to be known as someone who loves to help a colleague, and that is why others will also prefer to come to your aid when you need it.
Of course, on the playing fields, you will also encounter some irreconcilable opponents who are not willing to say a word to each other, let alone help each other with advice. However, fortunately, such people are not the majority.
Are you also ready to share your opinion and offer useful advice to others when you find it appropriate, even if you do not expect short-term benefits from it? In this case, you will gain a reputation as someone who is willing to selflessly contribute their experience and helpful suggestions for the common good. Offer your help whenever possible, and selflessly share your experience with others. It is a worthwhile investment, and I have yet to hear from any businessman who regretted it.

You take responsibility for unsuccessful presentations.

Taking personal responsibility for sales outcomes is an extremely important sales tool. It works so well that you will be surprised why you didn't actually incorporate this trick as a sales tool when you first heard about it. That's exactly what happened to me.

First of all, you must be firmly convinced that you can offer the potential buyer the most suitable solution to their problems. If you are not confident in this, then this trick, which we will discuss in more detail, won't help you either. If a potential client or anyone else asks you to tell them more about your company, sincerely and as convincingly as possible, tell them that you are proud to work for such a successful company as yours.

During a visit to a potential client, just before the conversation ends, ask them when it would be most convenient for you to deliver your product or start your service. Two things can happen: the person may respond "yes" and become your client, or they may decline your offer. If the latter happens to you, you must take responsibility for their negative decision.

Surprise!

My acquaintances, who are successful businessmen, use a special technique in such cases. They are noticeably surprised by the negative decision of the interlocutor and do not pretend otherwise. They are so confident in their company and know their interlocutor so well at that moment that they are genuinely taken aback by the negative response. Of course, you can do this too. For example, like this:

"Mr. Jones, I really don't know what else to say! I am confident that we can offer you the best service, that we have the most suitable prices, that we provide our clients with the most professional assistance, and that we enjoy a stellar reputation in our field. That's why I'm even more surprised that you're not accepting our offer. Clearly, I must have made a significant mistake during the presentation. That's why I'm asking you to tell me where I went wrong or where I didn't express myself clearly enough to indicate that my proposal is practically written on your skin, and I really wouldn't want to leave with the unpleasant feeling that I made a big mistake."

And what do you think the response will be?

If you were in his place, he would probably not hide his respect for someone who believes so strongly in what they do and who is brave enough to acknowledge their mistake.

The typical response you will hear after taking personal responsibility for the negative decision is likely to be something like: "No, no, Morin, our negative response has nothing to do with you personally. The reasons for our negative decision are as follows:..." Then you can expect the interlocutor to describe in detail the remaining obstacles and reservations, which is extremely useful information that you can use to your advantage.

He definitely delivers on his promises!

It is worth repeating once again: the surprise trick that I briefly introduced is initially effective, but keep in mind that you will have to prove that you can fulfill your promises. I would also like to point out another trap: you must resist the temptation to "always be right," which is something we all find difficult to resist once it gets hold of us.

But decide: do you prefer your "right" answer at any cost, or do you prefer to succeed in sales?

You are honest with yourself about the company you work for.

In my presentations and seminars, I often compare sales activities to war, emphasizing that in both fields, careful planning is critical; that in both the business world and in war, there are winners and losers; and that both require suitable ammunition and effective leadership. I could, of course, list a few more similarities, and when I discuss them, I never forget to emphasize that sales have some decisive advantages over war: it doesn't kill anyone, and we can change the "army" we fight for at our own will.

Take a closer look at your business, as well as at yourself. To effectively change your "army," you must first make an honest self-assessment. If you find yourself in a work environment that does not meet your personal criteria in terms of quality, ethics, and relationships with business partners, seriously consider moving elsewhere. Too often, salespeople persist in an "army" that is entirely unsuitable for them. The list of reasons they give is endless: I don't have enough time; I lack personal connections; it's not that bad here; I don't know other companies well enough to work there, and so on. But if we examine these excuses closely, we find that they are essentially empty and unconvincing.

There is a risk that even those salespeople who are otherwise capable of being highly persuasive are ready to sell themselves on one idea or another. If this idea turns out to be ineffective despite their expectations, they tend to fall into self-pity and self-loathing. That's why it's especially important for you to always strive to be completely honest with yourself about your own direction and, of course, the direction of your company.

Why? Because much of your career depends on it. You aim to build productive and mutually beneficial relationships with the people you meet in your business life. If you find that your work in sales does not support this, and if, on the contrary, you find that you are accumulating dissatisfied clients, you are better off reconsidering your goals.

Games.

Some salespeople try to play games with themselves. Specifically, they try to find rational explanations for a situation that is fundamentally irrational and manipulative, seeing it as something it is not and never will be. Don't join them, and don't fall into this cleverly set trap.

At every step, you must be firmly convinced of the rightness of what you are doing, and at every moment, you must be guided by the belief that all your efforts align with your value system. Regardless of how you set your goals, you need to be confident that they are worth achieving. You must know what benefits people can gain from working with you, and you must believe that your company's efforts are such that you can identify with them.

If this is not the case, you will gradually start to realize that success at work will not favor you much.

Tell everyone you meet who you work for and what you sell.
Why not?
Why not mention it to your doctor, electrician, or dentist? To the taxi driver who recently gave you a ride? To a friend from another company? To the passenger on the airplane? Neighbors? Members of the charity organization you support? The man sitting next to you at the football match?
Why not talk to each of these people, and others, with enthusiasm and pride about your profession? I'm not suggesting you persuade everyone you meet to buy something from you, but rather that you develop the habit of clearly and confidently telling everyone that you are a salesperson for XYZ company, which sells the best computers in the country. Accompany your statement with a casual smile and eye contact. More often than you think, you'll find that the person you're speaking to will admit that their company is considering buying computers...

The Secret.

In my opinion, too many salespeople feel a real reluctance to tell people what they do professionally. Perhaps the real reason for this unwarranted reluctance is that we often don't take as much pride in our work as, say, a surgeon, lawyer, editor, scientist, professor, or worker, who has no difficulty discussing their work in its true scale. You should be proud to be a salesperson, too. After all, our economy couldn't function without people who, like me, are involved in sales. I realize that every successful action I take in sales benefits everyone in some way. Am I proud of it? I admit that I am, and quite a lot!

You should think of your work the same way. If you need to change something to feel this way, do it without prejudice or reservations. Then, look people in the eye confidently and tell them who you work for and what you sell. Make it a habit. At first, it may feel challenging, but soon you'll naturally introduce yourself along with your profession and the company you work for. Recent research shows that a habit maintained for at least twenty-one consecutive days becomes second nature and is picked up subconsciously.

It's worth a try!

At the very least, start by introducing yourself to small groups of friends or people you know well enough to speak to comfortably, but who don't know what you do. But it's even better if, when you introduce yourself, you tell everyone what you do and for whom. It's definitely easier than you think, and you'll find that this method of introduction will bring you many benefits.

You keep your sense of humor.
Let's be honest: being a successful salesperson is no easy task. Surprisingly, however, this demanding profession can even bring joy because of its challenges. Based on my own experience, which I have accumulated over many years of working with different salespeople, I've come to the conclusion that laughter can be a great help. Salespeople rely on maintaining a good mood even more than those in other professions. However, it will be hard for you to maintain the image of a person who overcomes challenges with goodwill and a smile if you take yourself so seriously that you can't laugh lightly in the face of obstacles.

Let's look back for a moment. One of the strongest arguments against becoming a salesperson was certainly the film Salesman, which I watched many years ago. It's a black-and-white documentary that tells the story of three traveling salesmen, portraying their work as unfair and fraudulent—a job that no rational and honest person would willingly choose. For the reasons you can see, this film presents a real problem. The first reason is that it was watched by many people outside of sales, who formed a distorted and stereotypical view of my profession based on the film's portrayal. The other issue is that most people in sales haven't seen this movie, so they can't fully appreciate how destructive poor sales practices can be. This film actually serves as a very convincing example of how a salesperson, if they approach their work incorrectly, can be dangerous to both customers and themselves. If you are a salesperson, especially one who takes your work very, very seriously, this film will also leave a significant impression on you.

The salespeople featured in the film I mentioned make nearly all the mistakes I've highlighted in this book, plus one more: they disregard the needs and wishes of their customers, hold an extremely negative attitude towards their work, lie, and mislead potential buyers. They also show no interest in improving their incompetence.
However, they make another fundamental mistake that, if corrected, could easily help solve all the other issues. They take their work too seriously and never relax, not even for a moment. This makes it difficult to handle what are, in reality, extremely challenging problems.
If these challenges have become part of your daily sales routine.
They're even harder to overcome if you don't know how to relax now and then and manage to laugh a little—ideally, during your work.

Above All, You Are Important!

As a salesperson, you are too important a sales asset to neglect moments of relaxation and forget the need to stay calm, despite all the challenges chasing you. Today's catastrophe doesn't mean that the sun won't shine tomorrow. This is a message that the clumsy salespeople in the film never grasped and that eluded them at nearly every step.
Never count on not bearing personal responsibility for every workday, every month, and your entire career. After all, you're the person from whom customers expect the right answers, you're the one who professionally solves problems, and you also have to ask the most meaningful questions and be as precise as possible when giving advice. Relax, smile, and succeed! Remember, this is the only true path to success.

accept and use the above material.

---

1. **You convince people that they can trust you.**
Never take shortcuts that could damage your credibility—one of your strongest assets. Develop your leadership skills and build mutually beneficial, long-term partnerships.

2. **You ask the right questions.**
Simplify your work by asking straightforward questions that encourage the other person to talk about themselves. Then move on to the past, present, and future, and ask yourself "why" and "how" each time. Avoid getting caught up in secondary questions, as you are responsible for keeping the sales cycle moving forward smoothly and without unnecessary pauses.

3. **You take the initiative.**
At every stage of the sales cycle, let your conversation partner know where you are in the process, and don't be afraid to steer the discussion in the direction you need. If they have any questions or concerns, you'll hear about them in a timely manner, which is exactly what you want! When in doubt, take the initiative, but do so calmly and professionally.

4. **You engage the potential buyer.**
Never play "ping-pong" with the conversation by using their questions as your only guide. Instead, direct the discussion to areas where you feel most at home, and listen carefully when they start talking about themselves. In those moments, show them your full attention.

5. **You identify key requirements.**
The motto "Identify needs and meet them!" has its limitations. For most of us, the days when we could fully or even largely rely on the needs of existing clients are long gone. Identify the needs of more discerning clients who know that the choice is theirs.

---

6. **You count to three before surrendering to triumph.**
Do you believe you deserve success in sales? Maybe you're right, but take enough time to establish closer connections with your conversation partner and learn about their desires. Then suggest a personal meeting. Don't assume that success has simply fallen into your hands.

7. **You know how to rebrand your product or service.**
Can the product you offer only serve one purpose? Have you ever considered changing your product or service to achieve a new purpose? Could you offer the product or service differently or to a different group of people?

8. **Pretend to be a consultant (because you really are one).**
Don't improvise! If you need a little more time to prepare a suitable solution, take it. The whole point is in problem-solving, and you'll need to listen carefully before suggesting the most appropriate solution.

9. **From the very first meeting, you suggest the next one.**
Of all the advice in this book, this may be the simplest and easiest to follow. Don't argue—schedule meetings!

10. **You take notes.**
Taking notes during a meeting with a potential buyer helps you listen more attentively. Note-taking gives you credibility and encourages your conversation partner to open up more, allowing you to learn more than you otherwise would.

11. **With each new potential client, you create a personalized plan.**
For you, the meeting may seem routine, but your conversation partner might not have gone through the sales cycle with you before. Based on notes from previous meetings, create a customized plan specifically for them, remembering that you're acting like a doctor—don't rush the diagnosis!

12. **Ask for referrals.**
Don't be too timid or restrained; you simply can't afford it. Referrals are incredibly important for a successful career in sales. Always carry a stack of business cards and say to your conversation partner, "I'm sure there are people in your field who would benefit from discussing the product or service I offer. Could you name five such businesspeople I could speak with?"

Be bold about your company, remembering that there is a huge difference between enthusiasm and poorly concealed panic. Enthusiasm builds bridges, while panic destroys them.

14. **Give yourself due credit.**
Speak about yourself, but be humble. (Yes, these two concepts aren't mutually exclusive.) Express a sense of accomplishment, confidence, and flexibility. Highlight your previous successes without attempting to elevate yourself above your conversation partner. Aim to show especially those qualities characteristic of someone who knows how to make things happen effectively.

You tell the truth (it's easier to remember).
On average, we tell 200 "white" lies a day! Flattery and social conventions are one thing, but deceiving a conversation partner by promising a deadline you can't meet or guaranteeing a certain quality is quite another. Remember that your reputation is very valuable, so take care of it!

15. **You sell yourself to yourself.**
Motivate yourself! On your morning commute, if possible, avoid listening to the radio—listen instead to motivational tapes. Be consistent with your goals and rewards. Encourage yourself, leave yourself written reminders, and keep things in perspective.

Early hour, golden hour—start early and love it.
Before nine in the morning, so much can be accomplished! You can avoid talking to secretaries on the phone, cut and ease your path, and spare yourself frustration if you leave home an hour earlier than usual. This advice might seem a bit challenging, but give it a try. An early start to the workday will become a habit before you know it.

---

16. **You read professional publications (from your field and that of your clients).**
Read business newspapers and journals, as they are invaluable sources of data and information. You'll find everything in them, from minor insights to significant trends. Make the most of this opportunity.
The next day, highlight the essence of your visit.
After the initial visit, follow up with your prospective client by calling them or sending a brief note. Most people who consider this end up not finding the time for this extremely beneficial business step, but you can easily fit it into your schedule!

17. **You reach out to businesspeople and citizen groups.**
You can expect numerous benefits from boosting your confidence, which you gain especially when others regard you as an expert in your field (and you are one). On average, one in ten listeners will ask about the product or service you offer.
When the opportunity arises, you share your expertise with others.
"As in the forest, so out of it." It's a wise choice to offer assistance to others when they need it, and I have yet to hear of a salesperson who regretted such a decision.

18. **You take responsibility for unsuccessful presentations.**
Did they turn you down? Try something like this: "Mr. Jones, I honestly don't understand… I must have made a crucial mistake in my presentation that led you to reject my offer. I'm confident we can help you. Could you help me by pointing out where I went wrong? Perhaps it's just a misunderstanding?"
It's better to let go of your usual desire to always be right. Are you more interested in being right or succeeding in sales?

When it comes to the company you work for, you're honest with yourself and promote its reputation.
If you have to choose between fighting a losing battle for already lost generals and seeking another "army," choose the latter without hesitation.

19. **You tell everyone you meet about who you work for and what you sell.**
Why not proudly share what you do with everyone? This isn't the same as trying to convince everyone you meet to buy. Simply introduce yourself, your profession, and the company you work for.

20. **You maintain a sense of humor.**
Being a salesperson can be challenging, but that's exactly why you need to relax and laugh here and there. Remember, success tends to favor those who can stay cheerful and maintain a sense of humor, even in tough times.

Dear curious readers and future conquerors of the global sales markets,

In this desk and workbook, you will be able to read and master over twenty important and actionable skills in negotiation and sales preparation and execution. Read with pleasure and apply in practice, embodying your plans in sales.

useful knowledge.

www.ingramcontent.com/pod-product-compliance
Lightning Source LLC
Chambersburg PA
CBHW070131230526
45472CB00004B/1507